W9-CNO-468

ARKANSAS

Past and Present

Janey Levy

rosen publishing's
rosen
central

New York

Published in 2011 by The Rosen Publishing Group, Inc.
29 East 21st Street, New York, NY 10010

Copyright © 2011 by The Rosen Publishing Group, Inc.

First Edition

All rights reserved. No part of this book may be reproduced in any form without permission in writing from the publisher, except by a reviewer.

Library of Congress Cataloging-in-Publication Data

Levy, Janey.
Arkansas: past and present / Janey Levy.
    p. cm.—(The United States: past and present)
Includes bibliographical references and index.
ISBN 978-1-4358-9476-1 (library binding) — ISBN 978-1-4358-9504-1 (pbk.) — ISBN 978-1-4358-9538-6 (6-pack)
1. Arkansas—Juvenile literature. I. Title.
F411.3.L48 2011
976.7—dc22

                                                                2009052310

Manufactured in Malaysia

CPSIA Compliance Information: Batch #S10YA: For further information, contact Rosen Publishing, New York, New York, at 1-800-237-9932.

On the cover: Top left: A color print dramatically portrays the Battle of Pea Ridge (Benton County, Arkansas, 1862), one of the bloodiest Civil War battles west of the Mississippi River. Top right: A rice field in the Arkansas Delta. Rice is one of the state's most important crops. Bottom: The Buffalo River, which originates in the Ozark Plateau, was declared a national river in 1972. It is a prime example of the state's famously beautiful waterways.

Contents

Introduction   5

Chapter 1
The Geography of Arkansas   6

Chapter 2
The History of Arkansas   13

Chapter 3
The Government of Arkansas   19

Chapter 4
The Economy of Arkansas   25

Chapter 5
People from Arkansas:
Past and Present   31

Timeline   38

Arkansas at a Glance   39

Glossary   41

For More Information   42

For Further Reading   44

Bibliography   45

Index   46

Although Arkansas is landlocked, its lakes and rivers have done much to shape its history. Of special significance is the Mississippi River, which forms most of Arkansas's eastern border.

Introduction

Arkansas lies in the southern United States along the west bank of the Mississippi River. Its neighbors are Tennessee and Mississippi across the river, Louisiana to the south, Texas to the southwest, Oklahoma to the west, and Missouri to the north.

Arkansas's earliest inhabitants were the ancestors of modern Native Americans. These hunters and gatherers arrived more than twelve thousand years ago. By the time European explorers came, the Caddo, Osage, Quapaw, and other Arkansas Native Americans lived in villages and farmed. The state's name comes indirectly from the Quapaw. Native Americans to the north called them *akansea*, which means "south wind."

Spanish explorers came in the 1500s, followed by French explorers in the 1600s. The deadly diseases and new ways of life that they brought with them changed Arkansas forever.

Today, manufacturing is Arkansas's most important economic activity. Natural gas and oil are produced there. Big businesses, such as Walmart, have headquarters there.

Yet in some ways, Arkansas has not changed much. Its population remains small with fewer than three million inhabitants. Farming is still important. The state's beautiful landscape still draws people.

Despite its small population, Arkansas has been home to many well-known people, past and present. They include Quapaw leaders such as Heckaton; former president Bill Clinton; Sam Walton, Walmart's founder; and actors such as Mary Steenburgen.

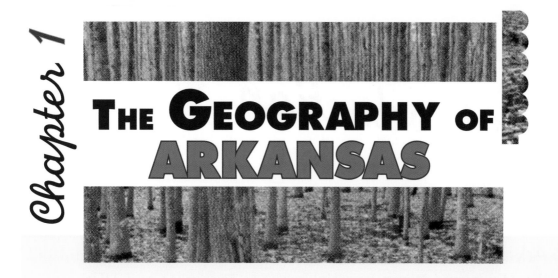

Chapter 1

THE GEOGRAPHY OF ARKANSAS

Arkansas is famous for the beauty of its mountains, valleys, and lowlands. Forests blanket about half the state. Lakes cover approximately 600,000 acres (243,000 hectares). About 9,000 miles (14,480 kilometers) of rivers and streams flow through Arkansas.

Arkansas is divided almost equally into highlands and lowlands. The highlands (uplands) in northwestern Arkansas include the Ozark Mountains (sometimes called the Ozark Plateau), the Ouachita Mountains, and the Arkansas River Valley. The lowlands in southeastern Arkansas include the Delta (also called the Mississippi Alluvial Plain), the Gulf Coastal Plain, and Crowley's Ridge. The variety and loveliness of these regions attract millions of visitors annually.

The Highlands

Arkansas's highlands formed hundreds of millions of years ago, when huge landmasses collided and pushed up layers of rock. This area is mountainous and heavily forested. Summers are warm, and winters are mild. The mild climate makes the highlands an excellent home for many kinds of wildlife.

The Ozark Mountains

The Ozarks have flat tops—plateaus—rather than the usual pointed peaks. Rivers have cut valleys into the plateaus, and limestone caves have formed inside them.

The average annual precipitation reaches 52 inches (110 centimeters) in some areas. Up to 6 inches (15 cm) of snow may fall during the winter. The average July temperature is 80 degrees Fahrenheit (27 degrees Celsius). January's average temperature is 36°F (2°C).

Pines and hardwood trees fill the forests. Wildflowers bloom from spring through fall, and plentiful mushrooms attract mushroom hunters.

The Ozark National Forest's brilliantly colored fall foliage provides a spectacular display of Arkansas's famous natural beauty.

The Ozarks shelter wildlife ranging from chipmunks to elk and black bears. There are songbirds, bald eagles, timber rattlesnakes, and trout. There are also rare animals such as the Ozark cavefish, the Ozark hellbender (a large water salamander), and the Ozark big-eared bat.

The Ouachita Mountains

Unlike the Ozarks, the Ouachitas have sharp peaks and ridges. Hot springs bubble to the surface in several places.

Black bears inhabit much of Arkansas. This photograph shows a man holding a cub from the Ozark National Forest, while a representative from the Arkansas Game and Fish Commission looks on.

The average annual precipitation is more than 48 inches (120 cm), with 6 inches (15 cm) of snow possible in the winter. The average July temperature exceeds 80°F (27°C). The average January temperature is 40°F (5°C).

Just as in the Ozarks, pines, hardwood trees, and wildflowers grow here. There are also wild berries.

Since the name "Ouachita" comes from a Native American word meaning "good hunting," it's not surprising that wildlife is abundant here. Game animals include deer, bear, turkeys, and quail. Songbirds, soaring birds, and water birds are also plentiful. Rare animals, like the bird-voiced tree frog, giant stag beetle, and western chicken turtle, live here, too.

The Arkansas River Valley

The Arkansas River Valley separates the Ozarks and the Ouachitas. Wide, flat land borders the river. Beyond are broad, hilly plains with scattered mountains. Surprisingly, the state's tallest mountain, Magazine Mountain, is here in the valley. There are swamps, too. The average annual precipitation may reach 52 inches (130 cm). July's average temperature is 80°F (27°C), while January's is 36°F (2°C). In addition to the plants found in the mountains, prairie grasses grow here.

Wildlife includes beavers and wild hogs, called razorbacks. The cricket frog, one of the smallest frogs in the United States, is found here. So is the largest frog, the American bullfrog. There are poisonous snakes, such as copperheads and cottonmouths, and rare animals like the trumpeter swan and prairie mole cricket.

The Lowlands

As their name suggests, the lowlands are low and mostly level land, with some hills and forests. Summers are warm to hot, and winters are very mild. Numerous kinds of wildlife inhabit the lowlands.

The Gulf Coastal Plain

The Gulf Coastal Plain began forming about 145 million years ago when the ocean covering the region withdrew. The retreating water left behind loose sand, gravel, silt, and clay. Bottomlands border the plain's rivers. Forests cover much of the bottomlands.

Water World

About 450 million years ago, Arkansas was a different—and much wetter—place than it is today. There was no dry land because an ocean covered the area that is now Arkansas! Unusual creatures filled this prehistoric ocean. There were trilobites (ancient invertebrates with exoskeletons, or skeletons covering their bodies), bryozoans (called moss animals because they resembled moss), brachiopods (invertebrates with two-part shells), echinoderms (relatives of starfish and sea urchins), and cephalopods (mollusks similar to squid). Ocean wildlife also included corals; snails; and strange, jawless, armored fish.

Around sixty-five million years ago, the ocean had withdrawn some but still covered about half the area that became Arkansas. A rich array of animals filled this ocean. There were snails, corals, and cephalopods, just as there were in the earlier ocean. There were also ancient forms of many common marine animals found in today's oceans, including oysters, barnacles, crabs, turtles, worms, and even crocodiles. Sharks, sawfish, and other fish swam in this ancient ocean. So, too, did now-extinct reptiles such as plesiosaurs and mosasaurs. The plesiosaur was a large marine reptile with fins shaped like paddles. The mosasaur was a large marine lizard that resembled a crocodile.

Today, Arkansas is mainly dry land. The prehistoric ocean and its creatures have long since disappeared. However, water is still an important feature of Arkansas. Bodies of water cover more than 1,000 square miles (2,500 square kilometers). Together with the rich array of surrounding wildlife, they contribute to the state's celebrated beauty. Visitors come to fish and boat in the sparkling waters of Arkansas's rivers, streams, and lakes, or to simply relax and enjoy nature's splendor. Hunters come for the wildlife around the waters. Arkansas has both cold and hot springs that draw visitors every year. Some come to enjoy the natural beauty and the activities available. Others come hoping the springs can cure health problems.

The average annual precipitation is 50 inches (130 cm). July's average temperature is 80°F (27°C), while January's average temperature ranges from 38°F (3°C) to 48°F (9°C).

Bottomland forests contain pines and hardwood trees. Wildflowers grow abundantly.

The region's wildlife ranges from rabbits to mountain lions. Wading birds are plentiful, but they must be careful: The reptiles include alligators! Among the rare animals are the southern crawfish frog and western slender glass lizard, a legless lizard that is often mistaken for a snake.

Cypress and tupelo trees grow in a hardwood swamp in White River National Wildlife Refuge.

The Delta

The Delta formed along with the Gulf Coastal Plain and thus shares many of its features, including the types of soil and the forested bottomlands. In addition, the Delta contains swamps.

The average annual precipitation exceeds 48 inches (120 cm). July's average temperature is above 82°F (28°C). The average January temperature ranges from 38°F (3°C) to 48°F (9°C).

Hardwood trees and swamp trees, such as cypress and tupelo, grow here. Wildflowers and prairie grasses are plentiful.

Wildlife ranges from tree frogs to alligators. Besides gentle deer and songbirds, there are bobcats and bears. The three-toed amphiuma, a salamander that is 3 feet (91 cm) long, lives here. Catfish swim in the waters. Rare animals include the American white pelican, paddlefish, and antlike tiger beetle.

Crowley's Ridge

Crowley's Ridge rises 200 feet (60 m) above the northeastern Delta. It's a narrow strip about 150 miles (240 km) long and from ½ to 20 miles (1 to 32 km) wide. Streams have cut steep valleys into its forested slopes.

The ridge formed during the Ice Age, when the courses of the Mississippi, Ohio, and Arkansas rivers differed from today. The flowing waters wore down most of the area, leaving only the ridge.

The average annual precipitation ranges from 44 inches (120 cm) to 52 inches (130 cm). July's average temperature exceeds 80°F (27°C), while January's average temperature is 34°F (1°C) to 42°F (6°C).

The forests have pines and hardwood trees. Vines, grasses, and wildflowers also grow there.

The immensely varied wildlife includes southern leopard frogs, nine-banded armadillos, songbirds, turkey vultures, opossums, and worm snakes. Rare animals, like the eastern spadefoot toad and American badger, inhabit the ridge.

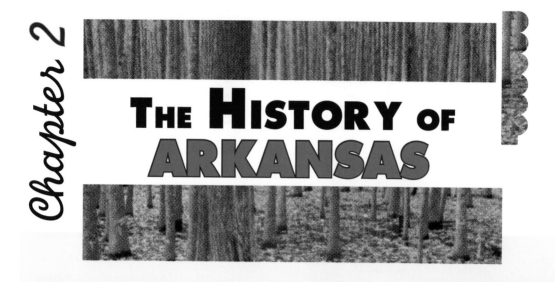

Chapter 2

THE HISTORY OF ARKANSAS

The Paleo-Indians, Arkansas's first people, arrived more than twelve thousand years ago. They were hunters and gatherers who moved often in search of food.

About six thousand years ago, the Archaic Period began. Archaic people were still hunters and gatherers. However, they also conducted long-distance trade. They kept dogs and valued them, for they buried their dogs like they did humans. About five thousand years ago, Archaic people began building mounds that were probably places for special events. About three thousand years ago, they began to grow some of their food. Their crops included gourds, squash, and sunflowers.

The Mississippian Period began about two thousand years ago. Mississippians were farmers, rather than hunters and gatherers. They raised crops such as maize (corn), beans, squash, and sunflowers. They had complex societies and religion.

By the time European explorers arrived in the 1500s, the three main Native American tribes in Arkansas were the Caddo, Osage, and Quapaw. The coming of Europeans changed their lives forever. Tens of thousands of Native Americans died from war and diseases that the Europeans brought with them. Most of the rest were forced off their land.

European Exploration and Settlement

An Italian artist produced this image of traditionally dressed Osage people for a book published in the 1820s or 1830s.

Spanish explorer Hernando de Soto and his men were the first Europeans to reach Arkansas. They passed through in 1541, and de Soto claimed the land for Spain. However, Spain didn't establish settlements, leaving the land open to other European explorers.

In 1673, French explorers Father Jacques Marquette and Louis Jolliet stopped in the area during their exploration of the Mississippi River. A few years later, in 1682, René-Robert Cavelier, Sieur (Lord) de La Salle claimed all the land around the Mississippi River for France. La Salle also granted to Henri de Tonti some choice land near the spot where the Arkansas and Mississippi rivers join.

In 1686, Tonti established a trading post on his land and called it Arkansas Post. It was the first permanent European settlement in Arkansas. Around 1720, about one hundred European settlers and their African slaves settled near Arkansas Post. Most soon left, but a few farmers stayed.

During the 1700s, control of Arkansas passed back and forth between France and Spain. Little settlement occurred during this period. Then, in 1803, the United States bought the Louisiana Territory from France. This huge expanse of land included the region that became Arkansas.

This print shows an 1863 Civil War battle in Arkansas. Union soldiers defeated Confederate troops at the Battle of Arkansas Post, also known as the Battle of Fort Hindman.

Arkansas as Part of the United States

From 1803 to 1812, the land that became Arkansas was simply part of the vast Louisiana Territory. In 1812, the Louisiana Territory was divided. Arkansas was included in the area that formed the Missouri Territory. The U.S. government created the Arkansas Territory in 1819. It included Arkansas and part of what is now Oklahoma. Arkansas wrote its first constitution in 1836 and became the twenty-fifth state in the United States that same year.

Arkansas Before and During the Civil War

When Arkansas became a state, the country was arguing about slavery. Some people, especially in the South, supported slavery because they believed it was necessary to maintain their way of life. Others, especially in the North, thought slavery was morally wrong and believed it should be abolished.

Life in Southeastern Arkansas

When Henri de Tonti established Arkansas Post in 1686, he chose a place that had been inhabited since the late Archaic Period. The Quapaw lived there in Tonti's time. They had been living there when de Soto traveled through in 1541 and when Marquette and Jolliet made their 1673 journey down the Mississippi River. The Quapaw were farmers who raised corn, beans, squash, pumpkins, and gourds. They also hunted and gathered wild foods. Men and women had different responsibilities. Men were hunters and warriors. Women were farmers and gatherers. The Quapaw lived in villages made up of longhouses. A longhouse was a large rectangular house occupied by several families. The longhouses surrounded a central plaza. The building nearest to the plaza was used for meetings of the village leader and council of elders.

Today, the area is both similar to and different from the land the Quapaw knew. It's part of Desha County, which has a small population (about fifteen thousand). Just as the Quapaw lived in villages, most people in the county today live in villages or on farms. There are few large towns. Farming remains important, but cotton, rice, and soybeans have replaced corn, beans, squash, pumpkins, and gourds as the major crops. Hunting is important, but not in the way it was for the Quapaw. The Quapaw hunted to provide for themselves. Today, Desha County attracts hunters from other places, and the money they spend contributes to the region's economy. There's some manufacturing (pet food, steel buildings, paperboard, and hospital garments), and the University of Arkansas at Monticello (UAM) College of Technology is located there. UAM offers degrees in agriculture, forest resources, business, computer information systems, nursing, education, and music.

Abraham Lincoln was elected president in 1860. Most Southerners expected him to abolish slavery. So Southern states began to withdraw from the nation and form a new country called the Confederate States of America. The Civil War erupted between the North and South in 1861. Arkansas joined the Confederacy that same year.

The North won the Civil War in 1865, and the nation became whole again. However, the government of Arkansas refused to rejoin the United States. The U.S. government finally put Arkansas under military control in 1867, and Arkansas rejoined the nation the following year.

Arkansas in the 1900s

Railroads connected Arkansas to the rest of the nation in the late 1800s and brought new prosperity to the state. In the early 1900s, two big events promised even greater prosperity. Oil was discovered near El Dorado in 1921, and the state's first large hydroelectric dam was built in 1924.

Other events destroyed that promise of prosperity. Crop prices fell after 1920. A terrible flood occurred in 1927, and drought came in 1930 during the Great Depression. The United States entered World War II in 1941. After the war ended in 1945, farming declined in importance. Many farmworkers lost their jobs and left the state. Then, in 1957, Arkansas entered the national spotlight in an unfavorable way. The U.S. Supreme Court had ruled that school segregation—the practice of having separate schools for whites and blacks—was unconstitutional. The court ordered Central High School in Little Rock to integrate, or admit both blacks and whites. At first, the state government refused to obey the court. The U.S. government finally forced the state to obey, but the situation was tense and scary for a while.

Arkansas earned quite a different place in the national spotlight in 1992. That year, Arkansas governor William Jefferson Clinton was elected president of the United States. He was extremely popular and was reelected in 1996.

Arkansas Since 2000

Since 2000, Arkansas has seen good and bad signs. The state has begun to attract new industries. The highlands have prospered, in part because many people from different parts of the country have chosen to retire there. An art museum that rivals some of the nation's greatest

Resistance to the integration of Little Rock Central High School was so fierce that soldiers had to protect black students when they entered the school.

is being built and is set to open to the public in 2011. Alice L. Walton, the daughter of Walmart founder Sam Walton, was the force behind Crystal Bridges Museum of American Art in Bentonville. Designed by world-famous architect Moshe Safdie, the museum has a collection of great works by American artists.

However, the state still faces challenges. Many parts of the Delta have lost residents, which has hurt the region's economy. The state suffers from air and water pollution, and it must reduce it. Arkansas's leaders must find a way to provide enough energy for the state, improve education, and strengthen the farm economy.

Chapter 3

THE GOVERNMENT OF ARKANSAS

When the Arkansas Territory was created in 1819, Arkansas Post was the largest town and became the capital. However, settlers mostly moved into other parts of the territory, and Arkansas Post became less important. Thus, in 1821, the capital moved to Little Rock. The city remains the state capital today.

Arkansas had to write a constitution in order to become a state. Territorial leaders wrote the first constitution in early 1836. It was short, not very detailed, and modeled on the U.S. Constitution. It recognized slavery; stated that the governor, legislators, and county officials were to be elected; and that other state officials, including judges, were to be chosen by the legislature. Governors had to be at least thirty years old and state residents for ten years. All free adult white men could vote.

New state constitutions were written several times during the 1800s. The current constitution was written in 1874, although it has been amended numerous times since then.

The Constitution of the State of Arkansas of 1874

The Civil War and the years following it made Arkansans distrustful of government, and the state constitution reflects that. People wanted greater control over their government and believed they would have more authority over local government than over a large, distant state government. These ideas guided state leaders when they met in Little Rock in 1874 to write a new constitution. They finished their work in the summer, and Arkansas voters approved the constitution in the fall. The 1874 constitution reduced the state government's power and increased the power of local governments. It increased the number of county officials. It sharply limited the state's power to tax and borrow money. It reduced the terms of office for elected state officials from four years to two (an amendment in 1992 changed the terms back to four years). It allowed the legislature to meet for sixty days every two years. It greatly reduced the governor's power.

Branches of Arkansas's Government

Like the U.S. government, Arkansas's government has three branches: the executive branch, the legislative branch, and the judicial branch. Each has its own functions and authority. A very detailed constitution and a system of checks and balances keep any one branch from gaining too much power.

Executive Branch

The job of the executive branch is to administer Arkansas's laws. The head of the executive branch is the governor, who is elected by the people. Other elected officials are the lieutenant governor, secretary of state, state attorney general, state auditor, state treasurer, and commissioner of state lands. All of these elected officials serve four-year terms and can serve for only two terms.

The governor's job is to help make laws, approve or veto bills, approve or veto the state budget, and appoint heads and members of various departments and commissions (many appointments must be approved by the state senate).

Until 1950, Arkansas didn't provide an official residence for the governor. However, work finally began on a residence, called the Governor's Mansion, in 1947. It was completed in January 1950, and the governor and his family moved into the mansion in February. It's located on Center Street in downtown Little Rock. It's surrounded by 8.5 acres (3.5 ha) that include several gardens.

The Arkansas Capitol building was modeled on the U.S. Capitol. It's even appeared in movies as a stand-in for the U.S. Capitol!

Legislative Branch

The legislative branch is the state's lawmaking body. The state's legislature is called the general assembly and has two parts, or houses: the Arkansas house of representatives and the Arkansas senate. The house of representatives has one hundred members who serve two-year terms. Each member represents about twenty-seven thousand people. The senate has thirty-five members who serve four-year terms. Each member represents about seventy-six thousand people.

The general assembly meets at the Capitol near downtown Little Rock. It meets for sixty days once every two years. This means that serving in the general assembly is a part-time job, so senators and

Arkansas's Capital

Arkansas Post, the first territorial capital, was a trading post, fort, and village. It was a rough-and-tumble frontier place with lots of violence and crime. Men carried guns and knives, and arguments quickly became fights.

The Arkansas Territory had about fourteen thousand settlers, including about two thousand slaves. Arkansas Post's population was about one thousand. Large areas of land were given to Native Americans between 1817 and 1820. However, settlers protested, and Native Americans were forced to move farther west.

When the legislature met in 1820, it decided to move the capital to Little Rock, where many wealthy and powerful settlers owned land. The move was made in 1821, and Little Rock has been the capital ever since.

Little Rock is on the Arkansas River, near the center of the state. It's a manufacturing center and the state's main trading and transportation center. It has been an important port city since 1969, when work on the Arkansas River made it possible for ships to reach the city. Many large companies, such as Dillard's department stores, have headquarters there. The city has the William J. Clinton Presidential Center and Library, the University of Arkansas at Little Rock, and other colleges. The city's population grew from about 50 in 1820 to more than 183,000 in 2000, and it became more varied. It has a large Spanish-speaking population, as well as Buddhists and Muslims.

The strikingly modern William J. Clinton Presidential Center and Library in Little Rock seems to float above the reflecting pool.

representatives have other jobs the rest of the time.

In addition to passing laws, the general assembly levies taxes and prepares the state budget.

Judicial Branch

The judicial branch interprets and enforces state laws. It consists of four levels of courts: city and district courts, circuit courts, the Arkansas court of appeals, and the Arkansas supreme court.

City courts hold trials for cases involving the breaking of city ordinances and crimes defined as misdemeanors (minor crimes) by state law.

Gardens surround the Governor's Mansion, which was built in a style inspired by the architecture of ancient Greece and Rome.

District courts hold trials for misdemeanor cases, civil (noncriminal) cases involving less than $5,000, and preliminary felony (major crime) cases. Circuit courts hold trials for criminal and civil cases, cases involving young people, and cases involving family matters.

The Arkansas court of appeals hears appeals from trial court judgments. It was created in 1978 to help the Arkansas supreme court, which had more cases than it could handle. Its twelve judges are chosen in nonpartisan elections to serve eight-year terms. Its judgments are final and can't be appealed to the Arkansas supreme court.

The Arkansas supreme court hears appeals from trial courts. Its seven judges are chosen in nonpartisan elections to serve eight-year terms. In addition to hearing appeals, it supervises all Arkansas courts and regulates the practice of law and the professional conduct of attorneys.

Local Governments

The chief executive officer in each of Arkansas's seventy-five counties is the county judge. The judge approves county expenses and heads the county legislature, which is called the quorum court. Other county officials are the assessor, circuit clerk, county clerk, medical examiner or coroner, sheriff, surveyor, treasurer, and collector. All county officials are elected to serve two-year terms.

The Saline County Courthouse, where the county judge's office is located, was begun in 1901 and completed in 1902.

Cities and towns have governments run by a mayor and council or council and manager. There are also special districts, such as school districts.

Chapter 4

THE ECONOMY OF ARKANSAS

Manufacturing is the most important economic activity in Arkansas, and food processing is the leading manufacturing activity. Other important manufactured goods include metal products and transportation equipment. Arkansas's gross domestic product (GDP) for 2008 was more than $98 billion. As of September 2009, almost 1.3 million people in the state had jobs. While Arkansas's GDP and number of employed people are small compared to many other states, it's important to remember that the state's population is small, too.

Manufacturing in Arkansas

Food processing, Arkansas's principal manufacturing activity, has a long history in the state. Poultry processing began in the early 1900s. One of the early poultry processing companies was Tyson Foods. Today, Tyson Foods is the most important manufacturer in Arkansas and one of the largest poultry and meat processors in the world. Its headquarters are in Bentonville.

Although Tyson Foods is probably Arkansas's best-known food processing company, the state has many others. One is the meat processing company Land O'Frost, which has headquarters in Searcy.

Tyson Foods celebrated the opening of a new research and development facility in 2007. Reporters who attended the event were served—naturally—chicken.

Another is sausage-maker Odom's Tennessee Pride, which has a plant in Little Rock. There's also De Wafelbakkers, which makes European-style waffles, pancakes, and French toast, and has its headquarters in North Little Rock.

A wide variety of other products are manufactured in Arkansas. Some people may be surprised to learn what other goods are produced in the state. For example, although people often associate car manufacturing with Detroit, Michigan, Arkansas is also involved in the automobile industry. Car parts are manufactured in the state. So are aircraft parts and rail-road cars. Other goods manufactured in Arkansas include metal products, chemical products, and paper products.

Other Parts of Arkansas's Economy

Riceland, in Stuttgart, is a farmers' cooperative for rice, soybean, and wheat farmers. About nine thousand farmers from Arkansas and the surrounding states belong to the cooperative.

Although manufacturing (especially food processing) and service industries make up the major portion of Arkansas's economy, they are certainly not the entire economy. Agriculture remains impor-tant, mining is a valuable part of the economy, and tourism makes a small but significant contribution.

Agriculture

Farms cover almost half of Arkansas's land area. More than half of the money generated by farms comes from livestock products. Young, tender chickens called broilers are the leading farm product. Other important livestock products include beef cattle, dairy prod-ucts, eggs, hogs, and turkeys. Crops are also important. The most valuable crops are cotton, rice, and soybeans. Arkansas is one of the leading cotton-growing states. It leads all other states in the produc-tion of rice. Soybeans are one of the most widely grown crops in

Arkansas's Economy in a Changing World

For thousands of years, Arkansas's economy was based on its abundant natural resources. The earliest people relied on the region's wealth of wild animals for hunting and fishing and wild foods for gathering. The state's natural waterways promoted trade, even during very early times. Over time, the rich soil and bountiful water supply fostered the growth of agriculture. Initially, the economy did not change much during the early period of European settlement. The region's rich natural resources attracted European settlers just as they had the earlier inhabitants. The earliest settlers, however, mostly saw in those resources the promise of riches, rather than a good place to settle permanently. They were mainly hunters and traders who sought to supply animal furs and skins to meet the growing demand for those goods. Over time, agriculture became an important part of the European settlers' economy just as it had been for the people of the Mississippian Period.

The development of the global economy has created both new competition and new opportunities. Cotton must now compete with foreign imports and man-made fibers. It's no longer as important to Arkansas's economy as it once was. Competition from crops grown in other states and countries has changed agriculture. Farming has become a big business. Large corporate farms have replaced small family farms. Agriculture's importance to Arkansas's economy has declined.

Beginning in the late 1900s, service industries became much more important to Arkansas's economy. Service industries are those that don't produce goods but provide some kind of service, such as entertainment, health care, or car repair. Hotels, restaurants, and retail trade are service industries. Arkansas's service industries include some important companies. Walmart, the world's largest retailer, has headquarters in Bentonville. Dillard's department stores has headquarters in Little Rock. Arkansas is also home to two big trucking companies: J. B. Hunt (in Lowell) and ABF Freight System (in Fort Smith).

Arkansas. Other important crops are corn, hay, and wheat.

Mining

A wide range of resources is mined in Arkansas. It may surprise some people to learn that fuels such as natural gas and petroleum, or oil, are the state's most important mined products. Another major product is bromine, which is used for dyes, medicines, pesticides, and water purifiers. Numerous kinds of stones are mined, including one called novaculite. This stone is used to make Arkansas whetstones, which are considered among the finest in the world.

Why does this young visitor look so happy? She discovered a large diamond at Crater of Diamonds State Park. She will take it home to Missouri with her.

Tourism

Tourism generated $5.6 billion in Arkansas in 2008. Most visitors come to enjoy the state's beautiful scenery. The highlands are especially popular with visitors, although people who come to hunt and fish go wherever they can find the wildlife they're seeking. Some visitors enjoy hiking and camping. Others like to visit the limestone caves. Bull Shoals Caverns were formed 350 million years ago. In Old Spanish Treasure Cave, visitors can see fossils from the ocean that once covered Arkansas. Inside Lost Valley Trail Cave, there's a waterfall that is 35 feet (nearly 11 m) high! Arkansas has dozens of state and national parks for visitors to enjoy. At Crater of Diamonds State Park, visitors can even hunt for diamonds and keep any that they find! Cities with springs, such as Hot Springs, Eureka Springs, and Mammoth Spring, draw many visitors and offer activities to please a variety of interests. Bentonville's Crystal Bridges Museum of American Art and Little Rock's William J. Clinton Presidential Center and Library will undoubtedly attract more and more visitors in the future. Arkansas's government is working hard to promote tourism and make people aware of the many attractions that the state has to offer.

Economic Progress in a Poor State

Arkansas has historically been a poor state with a small population and limited financial resources. It still faces many challenges to improving living conditions for its citizens. Arkansas has consistently had lower income per person than most other states in the United States. Yet in spite of economic problems that began around the world in 2008, the economy of Arkansas has shown positive signs. Per person income has grown fairly steadily since 2000, and it has grown at a faster rate than that of the United States as a whole. The state's GDP has grown since 2005. Arkansas's leaders and citizens are working hard to give their state a brighter future.

Chapter 5

PEOPLE FROM ARKANSAS:
PAST AND PRESENT

Over the centuries, Arkansas has been home to many famous people in many fields of endeavor. They have influenced not only Arkansas, but also the nation as a whole. The people listed here are only a few of Arkansas's celebrated residents.

Joey Lauren Adams (1971–) Joey Lauren Adams was born and grew up in North Little Rock, where she acted in local church plays. She moved to Los Angeles when she was seventeen to pursue an acting career. She has appeared on television and in more than thirty movies, including *Coneheads*, *Mallrats*, *Chasing Amy*, *Big Daddy*, and *The Break-Up*.

John Hanks Alexander (1864–1894) John Alexander was born in Helena to parents who were former slaves. He became the second African American to graduate from West Point and the first to have a regular command position in the U.S. Army. In 1918, a military installation at Newport News, Virginia, was named Camp Alexander in his honor.

Daisy Gaston Bates (1914–1999) Daisy Bates was born in Huttig. She spent her life fighting for the civil rights of

31

When this photograph was taken in 1981, Sarah Caldwell was nationally famous. She had appeared on *Time* magazine's cover and received the first Kennedy Center Award for Excellence.

African Americans. She was an adviser and friend to the black students who integrated Little Rock Central High School in 1957. Later, she and her husband published an African American newspaper.

Sarah Caldwell (1924–2006) Sarah Caldwell grew up in Fayetteville and attended Hendrix College in Conway and the University of Arkansas. A gifted musician, she was giving public concerts by the time she was ten. She founded the Opera Company of Boston and was the first woman to conduct New York's Metropolitan Opera.

Glen Campbell (1936–) This famous pop and country singer was born in Delight. His hit songs include "By the Time I Get to Phoenix," "Wichita Lineman," and "Rhinestone Cowboy." He also had his own television shows and appeared in movies such as *True Grit* and *Any Which Way You Can.*

Johnny Cash (1932–2003) This famous country singer was born in Kingsland. His parents were poor farmers. His first hit was "Folsom Prison Blues" in 1956. He later appeared in movies and on television. He won eleven Grammy Awards for his music and is a member of the Country Music Hall of Fame and the Rock and Roll Hall of Fame.

Ronnie Dunn (1953–) Ronnie Dunn is a famous country singer who was born in El Dorado. He is one half of the singing group Brooks and Dunn. In 1996, the Country Music Academy named the duo Entertainers of the Year.

Charlaine Harris (1951–) This noted writer works out of her home in Magnolia. She has written a number of bestselling books, including *Dead Until Dark* and *Dead and Gone. True Blood*, the HBO television series about vampires, is based on her series of books about vampires.

John H. Johnson (1918–2005) This publisher was born in Arkansas City. He founded *Ebony* and *Jet* magazines and was the first African American to be named to *Forbes*'s list of the four hundred richest Americans. He was awarded the Medal of Freedom by President Bill Clinton in 1996.

Arkansas Leaders

Although people may not realize it, Arkansas has produced many great leaders. In fact, there have been so many that it's only possible to list a few of them here.

Hattie Caraway (1878–1950) Hattie Caraway settled in Jonesboro with her husband in 1902. She was the first woman ever elected to the U.S. Senate, the first to head a Senate committee, and the first to become a senior senator.

William Jefferson Clinton (1946–) Born in Hope, Bill Clinton grew up in Hot Springs. He was Arkansas's attorney general (1976–1978), then governor (1978–1980,1982–1993). He was U.S. president from 1993 to 2001.

J. William Fulbright (1905–1995) J. William Fulbright grew up in Fayetteville. As a U.S. senator (1945–1974), he established the Fulbright Fellowship program to support student and teacher exchange between the United States and other countries.

Heckaton (?–1842) Heckaton was the main Quapaw chief in Arkansas by 1816. Heckaton used peaceful means to try to protect Quapaw land rights. In spite of his heroic efforts, the Quapaw were forced out in 1834.

Mike Huckabee (1955–) Mike Huckabee was born in Hope. He was the governor of Arkansas from 1996 to 2007 and ran unsuccessfully for president in 2008.

Hattie Caraway poses in her office at the U.S. Capitol in 1940.

Cliff Lee (1978–) Cliff Lee was born in Benton and still lives there. The noted pitcher began his career with the Montreal Expos and now plays for the Philadelphia Phillies. In 2008, he was named the American League Cy Young Award winner.

Mark Martin (1959–) Mark Martin was born and grew up in Batesville. In his early teens, he began racing on dirt tracks in Arkansas. He began racing in NASCAR in 1981 and has won almost one hundred races.

Mark Martin takes a thoughtful moment beside his racecar before a NASCAR race.

Isaac C. Parker (1838–1896) Isaac C. Parker was a U.S. judge for the Western District, which included Arkansas, from 1875 to 1896. His courtroom was in Fort Smith. He sentenced so many men to be hung that he was known as the Hanging Judge.

Scottie Pippen (1965–) This famous professional basketball player was born in Hamburg. He played for the Chicago Bulls, where he and teammate Michael Jordan led the Bulls

to six national champion-
ships. He is considered one
of the best all-around play-
ers of all time.

**Art Porter Sr. (1934–
1993)** Art Porter Sr. was a
jazz musician who was born
in Little Rock and spent his
life there. He founded a
band called the Art Porter
Trio in 1962. Although he
was famous, he chose to stay
in Little Rock, where he
performed and taught music.

Scottie Pippen prepares to take a free throw during a game between the Chicago Bulls and the Miami Heat.

Bass Reeves (1838–1910)
Bass Reeves was born a
slave in Crawford County.
The slaveholders with
whom he lived, the Reeves family, moved to Texas in 1846.
He fled to Indian Territory (Oklahoma) during the Civil War.
After the war, he returned to Crawford County. He became
the first African American west of the Mississippi River to be
a U.S. deputy marshal. He was known for being dependable
and hardworking. He was made a member of the National
Cowboy Hall of Fame in 1992.

Mary Steenburgen (1953–) An acclaimed actress, Mary
Steenburgen was born in Newport and grew up in North

Little Rock. She has appeared on television and in numerous movies. She won an Academy Award for *Melvin and Howard* in 1981. Among her other films are *Parenthood, Back to the Future III,* and *Elf.*

Billy Bob Thornton (1955–)
Billy Bob Thornton was born in Hot Springs. He became famous for his acting as the lead character in the 1996 movie *Sling Blade.* Some of his other movies are *Armageddon, A Simple Plan, Monster's Ball, The Man Who Wasn't There, Love Actually,* and *Eagle Eye.*

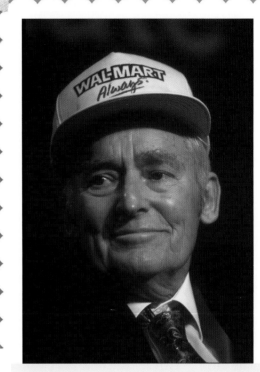

Sam Walton is shown here shortly before his death in 1992. By this time, Walmart was the nation's largest retailer.

Sam Walton (1918–1992)
The founder of Walmart was born in Newport. He opened his first Walmart in Rogers in 1962. By the time he died, there were 1,600 Walmarts in thirty-two states, and annual sales exceeded $44 billion.

Timeline

10,000 BCE Paleo-Indians arrive.

1541 Hernando de Soto and his men become the first Europeans to see Arkansas; de Soto claims the land for Spain.

1673 French explorers Father Jacques Marquette and Louis Jolliet arrive.

1682 René-Robert Cavelier, Sieur de La Salle claims the land for France.

1686 Henri de Tonti establishes Arkansas Post.

1803 The United States buys Louisiana Territory, including Arkansas, from France.

1812 Arkansas becomes part of Missouri Territory.

1819 Arkansas Territory is created.

1821 The territorial capital moves from Arkansas Post to Little Rock.

1836 Arkansas writes its first constitution and becomes the twenty-fifth state.

1861–1865 Arkansas sides with the Confederacy during the American Civil War.

1868 Arkansas rejoins the United States.

1874 Arkansas writes its current constitution.

1921 Oil is discovered in Arkansas.

1927 A terrible flood occurs in the state.

1930 A drought hits Arkansas.

1945 Manufacturing becomes more important than agriculture.

1957 A school integration controversy erupts in Little Rock.

1992 Arkansas governor Bill Clinton is elected president of the United States.

Late 1900s Service industries become an important part of the economy.

Early 2000s Arkansas's economy grows.

2010 The Crystal Bridges Museum of American Art is under construction in Bentonville.

State motto:	*Regnat Populus* ("The People Rule")
State capital:	Little Rock
State flag:	A white diamond outlined in blue appears on a red field with the word "Arkansas." Twenty-five white stars on the blue band represent Arkansas as the twenty-fifth state. The four blue stars stand for the four countries that have ruled the state.
State seal:	An eagle grasps an olive branch and arrow. Its beak holds a scroll with the state motto. A shield on its chest shows items important to the state's history. Figures of Liberty, Mercy, and Justice flank the eagle.
State flower:	Apple blossom
State fruit or vegetable:	South Arkansas vine-ripe pink tomato
State tree:	Pine
State bird:	Mockingbird
Statehood date and number:	June 15, 1836; twenty-fifth state
State nickname:	The Natural State
Total area and U.S. rank:	53,187 square miles (137,754 sq km); twenty-seventh-largest state

State Flag

State Seal

Population:	2,673,000
Highest elevation:	Magazine Mountain, at 2,753 feet (839 m) above sea level
Lowest elevation:	Near the Ouachita River at the Arkansas-Louisiana border, at 55 feet (17 m) above sea level
Major rivers:	Mississippi River, Arkansas River, Red River, Ouachita River, White River
Major lakes:	Lake Chicot, Lake Catherine, Lake Hamilton, Lake Ouachita, Beaver Lake, Bull Shoals Lake, Norfork Lake, Table Rock Lake, Big Maumelle Lake, Nimrod Lake
Highest recorded temperature:	120°F (49°C) at Ozark, on August 10, 1936
Lowest recorded temperature:	–29°F (–34°C) in Benton County, on February 13, 1905
Origin of state name:	From the name used for the Quapaw by Native Americans to the north: *akansea*, meaning "south wind"
Chief agricultural products:	Cotton, rice, soybeans, livestock, dairy products
Major industries:	Food processing, and metal, chemical, and paper products

Mockingbird

Apple blossom

GLOSSARY

abolish To do away with.

alluvial Having to do with clay, silt, sand, gravel, or other matter deposited by flowing water.

architect A person who designs buildings and advises in their construction.

auditor Someone whose job it is to examine and confirm financial accounts.

bottomlands Flat, low-lying lands along a river or other waterway.

collide To crash into.

commissioner The person in charge of a government department.

constitution A written document that sets up the principles and laws for a state or country's government.

delta A roughly triangular area of land at the mouth of a river.

drought A very long period of dryness that harms crops.

Great Depression A worldwide period of economic problems during the 1930s, when many people were without jobs and there was a low level of business activity.

gross domestic product (GDP) The total value of all goods and services produced in a state or country.

hydroelectric Having to do with the production of electricity by waterpower.

invertebrates Animals that don't have a backbone.

judicial Having to do with the court system.

legislators The people who serve in a state or country's lawmaking body.

nonpartisan Free from association with political parties.

ordinances Town or city laws.

plateau A wide area of flat, level land that is much higher than the land around it.

precipitation Any form of moisture that falls from the sky, including rain and snow.

preliminary Having to do with the beginning stage of something.

prosperity The condition of flourishing.

retail trade The sale of goods in small amounts to those who will use these goods.

ridge A long series of hilly or mountainous crests.

soybeans Beans originally from Asia that are high in protein and oil.

unconstitutional Not in keeping with the constitution of a state or nation.

veto To refuse to approve a legislative bill, thus preventing it from becoming a law.

whetstones Stones used to sharpen knives and other tools.

Arkansas Department of Parks and Tourism

1 Capitol Mall

Little Rock, AR 72201

(501) 682-7777

Web site: http://www.arkansas.com

The Department of Parks and Tourism provides information to visitors and residents about Arkansas's regions and parks, events and activities, places to stay, and planning a trip. Its Web site also has information about the state's history and famous people from Arkansas.

Arkansas Historic Preservation Program

1500 Tower Building

323 Center Street

Little Rock, AR 72201

(501) 324-9880

Web site: http://www.arkansaspreservation.org

This program identifies, evaluates, registers, and preserves the state's historic and cultural resources and seeks to educate future generations of Arkansans about the value of these resources.

Arkansas Natural Heritage Commission (ANHC)

1500 Tower Building

323 Center Street

Little Rock, AR 72201

(501) 324-9619

Web site: http://www.naturalheritage.org

Since 1973, the ANHC has been working to protect Arkansas's land and wildlife and to educate people about the state's natural variety.

Delta Cultural Center

141 Cherry Street

Helena, AR 72342

(870) 338-4350

Web site: http://www.deltaculturalcenter.com

The Delta Cultural Center is a museum dedicated to the history of the Arkansas Delta. The museum interprets the Delta's history through exhibits, educational programs, annual events, and guided tours.

Historic Arkansas Museum

200 E. Third Street

Little Rock, AR 72201

(501) 324-9351

Web site: http://www.arkansashistory.com

The museum grounds include a pre–Civil War neighborhood, including the oldest home still standing in Little Rock and the site where William Woodruff once printed the *Arkansas Gazette*. Inside the museum, visitors can see art and objects made in Arkansas or visit the interactive gallery.

Old State House Museum

300 W. Markham

Little Rock, AR 72201

(50) 324-9685

Web site: http://www.oldstatehouse.org

Set in the oldest surviving state capitol west of the Mississippi River, the Old State House Museum is a National Historic Landmark. It overlooks the Arkansas River and houses a multi-media museum of Arkansas state history.

Web Sites

Due to the changing nature of Internet links, Rosen Publishing has developed an online list of Web sites related to the subject of this book. This site is updated regularly. Please use this link to access the list:

http://www.rosenlinks.com/uspp/arpp

Altman, Linda Jacobs, Ettagale Blauer, and Jason Laure. *Arkansas* (Celebrate the States). 2nd ed. Tarrytown, NY: Marshall Cavendish Children's Books, 2008.

Arnold, Morris S. *Rumble of a Distant Drum: The Quapaws and Old World Newcomers, 1673–1804*. Fayetteville, AR: University of Arkansas Press, 2007.

Blashfield, Jane F. *When Life Flourished in Ancient Seas: The Early Paleozoic Era* (Prehistoric North America). Mankato, MN: Heinemann-Raintree, 2005.

Carlson, Bruce. *Ghosts of the Ozarks: A Collection of Ghost Stories from the Ozark Mountains*. Wever, IA: Quixote Press, 2004.

Ficky, Brenda. *Whispering Darkness*. Frederick, MD: PublishAmerica, 2007.

Hanley, Ray, and Steven Hanley. *Main Street Arkansas: The Hearts of Arkansas Cities and Towns—As Portrayed in Postcards and Photographs*. Little Rock, AR: Butler Center for Arkansas Studies, 2009.

King, David C. *Arkansas* (It's My State!). New York, NY: Benchmark Books, 2007.

King, David C. *First People: An Illustrated History of American Indians*. New York, NY: Dorling Kindersley, 2008.

Lee, Sally. *Sam Walton: Business Genius of Wal-Mart* (People to Know Today). Berkeley Heights, NJ: Enslow Publishers, 2007.

Love, Berna. *Arkansas Indians: Learning and Activity Book*. Little Rock, AR: Butler Center for Arkansas Studies, 2007.

Macaulay, Ellen. *Arkansas* (From Sea to Shining Sea). New York, NY: Scholastic, 2009.

Mason, Richard. *The Red Scarf*. Atlanta, GA: August House Publishers, 2007.

McPherson, Stephanie Sammartino. *Bill Clinton* (History Maker Biographies). Minneapolis, MN: Lerner Publishing Group, 2008.

Murdoch, David S. *North American Indian* (DK Eyewitness Books). New York, NY: Dorling Kindersley, 2005.

Olien, Rebecca. *Arkansas* (Land of Liberty). Mankato, MN: Capstone Press, 2003.

Prentzas, G. S. *Arkansas* (America the Beautiful). New York, NY: Scholastic, 2009.

Smith, Rich. *Arkansas* (The United States). Edina, MN: ABDO Publishing, 2009.

Woodall, William. *Cry for the Moon*. Antoine, AR: Jeremiah Press, 2009.

BIBLIOGRAPHY

Arkansas Constitutional Convention. "Constitution of the State of Arkansas of 1874." Little Rock, AR: 1874.

Arkansas Game and Fish Commission. "Wildlife & Conservation." 2009. Retrieved November 6, 2009 (http://www.agfc.com/wildlife-conservation).

Blevins, Brooks. *Arkansas/Arkansaw*. Fayetteville, AR: University of Arkansas Press, 2009.

Central Arkansas Library System. "The Encyclopedia of Arkansas History and Culture." 2009. Retrieved October 31, 2009 (http://www.encyclopediaofarkansas.net).

Clark, David W., Steffany C. White, Annalea K. Bowers, Leah D. Lucio, and Gary A. Heidt. "A Survey of Recent Accounts of the Mountain Lion (*Puma concolor*) in Arkansas." Little Rock, AR: University of Arkansas at Little Rock, Department of Biology, 2000.

Coleman, Roger E. "The Arkansas River and the Development of Arkansas Post." Arkansas Post National Memorial, 1991. Retrieved November 6, 2009 (http://www.nps.gov/archive/arpo/history/coleman.htm).

Desha County. "About Desha County." Retrieved November 8, 2009 (http://www.deshaark.com/about_desha_county.shtml).

Farabee, M. J. "Paleobiology: The Early Paleozoic." Online Biology Book, 2001. Retrieved November 1, 2009 (http://www.emc/Maricopa.edu/faculty/farabee/BIOBK/BioBookPaleoo3.html).

Kazlev, M. Alan. "The Paleozoic—3." Palaeos, 2002. Retrieved November 1, 2009 (http://www.palaeos.com/Paleozoic/Paleozoic3.html).

Kennedy, Randy. "Crystal Bridges Museum of American Art in Arkansas Names a New Director." *New York Times*, August 18, 2009, p. C3.

McPeake, Rebecca, Don White Jr., and Rick Eastridge. "Encountering Black Bears in Arkansas." Little Rock, AR: University of Arkansas Cooperative Extension Service Printing Services, n.d.

Watt, Christopher L., Philip A. Tappe, and Mark F. Roth. "Concentrations of American Alligator Populations in Arkansas." *Journal of the Arkansas Academy of Science*, Vol. 56, 2002, pp. 243–249.

Williams, C. Fred, S. Charles Bolton, Carl Moneyhon, and LeRoy T. Williams, eds. *A Documentary History of Arkansas*. Fayetteville, AR: University of Arkansas Press, 2005.

Wilson, Carrie, and George Sabo III. "Historic Native Americans: The Quapaw Indians." Arkansas Archeological Survey, 2001. Retrieved October 31, 2009 (http://www.uark.edu/depts/contact/quapaw.html).

A

ABF Freight System, 28
Academy Awards, 37
Adams, Joey Lauren, 31
Alexander, John Hanks, 31
Arkansas
  economy of, 5, 16, 17, 18, 25–30
  geography of, 5, 6–12
  government of, 19–24
  history of, 5, 10, 13–18
  people from, 5, 31–37
Arkansas River, 12, 14, 22

B

Bates, Daisy Gaston, 31–32
Brooks and Dunn, 33
Bull Shoals Caverns, 29

C

Caddo Indians, 5, 13
Caldwell, Sarah, 32
Camp Alexander, 31
Campbell, Glen, 33
Caraway, Hattie, 34
Cash, Johnny, 33
Civil War, 17, 19, 36
Clinton, Bill, 5, 18, 22, 30, 33, 34
Country Music Academy, 33
Country Music Hall of Fame, 33
Crater of Diamonds State Park, 30
Crystal Bridges Museum of American Art,
  18, 30
Cy Young Award, 35

D

de Soto, Hernando, 14, 16
De Wafelbakkers, 26

Dillard's department stores, 22, 28
Dunn, Ronnie, 33

E

Ebony magazine, 33
Eureka Springs, 30

F

Forbes magazine, 33
Fulbright, J. William, 34
Fulbright Fellowship, 34

G

Grammy Awards, 33
Great Depression, 17

H

Harris, Charlaine, 33
HBO, 33
Heckaton, 5, 34
Hendrix College, 32
Hot Springs, 30, 34, 37
Huckabee, Mike, 34

J

J. B. Hunt Co., 28
Jet magazine, 33
Johnson, John H., 33
Jolliet, Louis, 14, 16
Jordan, Michael, 35

L

Land O'Frost, 25
La Salle, René-Robert Cavelier, Sieur de, 14
Lee, Cliff, 35
Lincoln, Abraham, 17

Little Rock Central High School, 17, 32
Lost Valley Trail Cave, 29

M

Magazine Mountain, 9
Mammoth Spring, 30
Marquette, Father Jacques, 14, 16
Martin, Mark, 35
Medal of Freedom, 33
Metropolitan Opera, 32
Mississippi River, 5, 12, 14, 16, 36

N

NASCAR, 35
National Cowboy Hall of Fame, 36

O

Odom's Tennessee Pride, 26
Old Spanish Treasure Cave, 29
Opera Company of Boston, 32
Osage Indians, 5, 13
Ouachitas Mountains, 6, 7–9
Ozark Mountains, 6, 7, 8, 9

P

Paleo-Indians, 13
Parker, Isaac C., 35
Pippen, Scottie, 35–36
Porter Sr., Art, 36

Q

Quapaw Indians, 5, 13, 16, 34

R

Reeves, Bass, 36
Rock and Roll Hall of Fame, 33

S

Safdie, Moshe, 18
Steenburgen, Mary, 5, 36–37

T

Thornton, Billy Bob, 37
Tonti, Henri de, 14, 16
Tyson Foods, 25

U

University of Arkansas, 16, 22, 32
U.S. Constitution, 19
U.S. Supreme Court, 17

W

Walmart, 5, 18, 28, 37
Walton, Alice L., 18
Walton, Sam, 5, 18, 37
William J. Clinton Presidential Center and
    Library, 22, 30
World War II, 17

About the Author

Janey Levy, the author of more than one hundred books for young readers of all ages, is an editor and writer who lives in Colden, New York. Her mother was born and raised in Arkansas and shared many stories of her childhood there. Levy also has many of her own memories of Arkansas from visits to family members there while she was growing up.

Photo Credits

Cover (top, left), pp. 15, 34 Library of Congress Prints and Photographs Division; cover (top, right) Clint Spencer/Photodisc/Getty Images; cover (bottom), p. 24 © www.istockphoto.com/David H. Lewis; pp. 3, 6, 13, 19, 25, 31, 38 © www.istockphoto.com/Clint Spencer; p. 4 © GeoAtlas; p. 7 © Tom Till/SuperStock; pp. 8, 18, 26, 29 © AP Images; p. 11 Joel Sartore/National Geographic/Getty Images; p. 14 Private Collection/The Stapleton Collection/Bridgeman Art Library; p. 21 Shutterstock.com; p. 22 Alex Wong/Getty Images; p. 23 cnstravelpix/Newscom.com; p. 27 © Robert King/Zuma Press; p. 32 Bachrach/Hulton Archive/Getty Images; p. 35 Darrell Ingham/Getty Images; p. 36 Al Messerschmidt/WireImage/Getty Images; p. 37 Luke Frazza/AFP/Getty Images; p. 39 (left) Courtesy of Robesus, Inc.; p. 40 (left) http://en.wikipedia.org/wiki/File:Mimus_polyglottos_adult_01_cropped.jpg; p. 40 (right) http://en.wikipedia.org/wiki/File:Appletree_bloom_l.jpg.

Designer: Les Kanturek; Editor: Kathy Kuhtz Campbell;
Photo Researcher: Amy Feinberg